AF410442

Whispers Of The Wind

Bluebird's song, Volume 1

Tinaye Makwanise

Published by Bluebird, 2024.

WHISPERS OF THE WIND

First edition. February 26, 2024.

ISBN: 979-8224292561

Written by Tinaye Makwanise.

Table of Contents

A walk alone

A walk alone I will take
I won't look back at the pack
For others I did toil
But only myself did I soil
They won't ask where I went
They never noticed where I sat
At the mountain's peak I will be seen
Away from scratching their backs
They will be dwarfs in my songs of great heights
And where my name is in the books they will not be found

Brother

Footsteps always sounded mildly behind me
this was the source of my bravery
Your ears were a net
that caught my every idea
Sometimes big
at times fresh
at most small and malnourished

In the rain we ran
in the sun we strolled
wherever the wind blew us we went

When I wanted to find myself
all I did was look for you
Like tongs we held the world together
Like scissors we cut through
The future I envisioned was the reflection of yours

Long had the world stopped to get between us
as it had realized the space between us was non-existent
These were our thoughts
The world proved them to be mere opinions

Miles from being facts

The walk you took
turned out to be a journey to the sun
and long I waited for your return
You had taken what was mine
in the thought that it was yours
Forsaking the you around me
while salvaging the little of me you had left behind
I returned to the place I thought I knew
Incomplete
What they called hills appeared as mountains
Gentle winds had become storms
even the stream now had current that befitted a river

Head bowed I fell on my knees and let out a cry
for I finally believed
my brother had left me

Flying to the sun

From above I see how my world could have been
I never belonged down there with only a place to rest my head
nowhere to put my wings
No one pointed me in the direction I am taking
None of them have been there before
Blinded by its sight I can only hear where I am going
It calls out to me like a mother to a lost child
Rumour has it that my destination burns visitors, likely I am not
one
No one really knows the labours of flying to the sun

Painful Longing

I don't think of you all the time
But when I do I don't stop
When I am cold I wonder if you are warm
When I am asleep I dream of you awake
Despite all this longing
I am glad you are faraway
I breathe better this way

Sweet illusions

Your figure forms as the music plays in my head
Thoughts of you then flood and I'm soon overwhelmed
At Least here you are mine with open arms
Reality slowly drains away the nice thoughts
Leaving behind the bitter truth
Like a river to the ocean again and again
I will never let you go
I can't

My heart is dying

Some see me singing but truly I've been crying
Don't say life is all about trying
I tried and it left my heart frying
Forget about what I said before I've been lying
I've decided to let myself loose from the knots I've been tying
I've tried my best don't you dare tell me about timing
Despite the work I put in
It really didn't work here I am sighing
I've finally sunk my plane it turned out to be a boat
So why did it I feel like flying
With all emotions shrinking I don't need a doctor to know the
heart is dying

I have forgotten everything come back

Guilt had its hands around your neck
To your legs you trusted your future
Never did you look back
Your footprints I did follow and you I did see
No fiery words did I hold
Nor did my eyes twinkle with vengeance
For a different fire burned within me
As you froze to the ghost before you
I whispered life back into you
I have forgotten everything come back

Afraid of love

My words were too warm
You chose the cold outside
Even with your eyes closed
You still saw yourself by my side
Afraid of melting into my arms
Afraid of the great joy that would bring
You stopped answering the door
Burnt my letters and refused my flowers
How long would you shelter your eagle from the sky

Disloyal Hands

A voice once told me to fear what I could control over what I
could not
In this new light I gave trust to whoever asked for it
I grew numb to the many spears that found rest on my back
From only one person did I withhold my trust
With a reflection in the mirror and a shadow behind him at day
His promises in my ears were like the words of an infant
His pledges like the yawning of the elderly
I never blamed him for I understood why
If I could warn you of the fate that befell your agreements I
would
But predictable is one thing he is not

Father

We never saw things in the same light
You looked down on me as if I was in the dark
I understood everything but you were too high up to bend
down and listen
You argued for sport I defended in the hope that we would both
win
You often thought you were right
I was hardly wrong
You were my father and I was your son

Fire for the night

A hunt for wood is how it began
running against time for night was coming when the hunter
would become prey
Of all shapes and sizes the forest gave up
Soggy and inflammable I left those behind
Prickly thorns were the surface of others yet I daringly took
them along
Gathered in a heap they stood majestically mocking the
Mammoth task that awaited them
As the first flames danced devouring the bark and crackling in
satisfaction
It seemed as if survival was imminent
The shades of yellow gave me an enveloping sensation
I let go of my eyelids and drifted in contentment
Half a moon through the night as the hissing grew faint
Only a handful lay there glowing in the ashes
What befell the forest I had gathered
No huff could save nature's blanket
Cuddled into a ball I drew near to the last of the flickers
Sighing for it wouldn't hold the night

Loneliness her animal

I could not make of the creature you left me
Until it grew in your prolonged absence
There was no need for introductions
The beast felt part of me yet against me
As a phantom it reappeared before me when I tried to run
Encircling me when my legs gave up the chase
I covered my eyes from the great emptiness that reflected from
its own
From my friends it did shy away waiting for the night when I
would be alone

Stop running

We have chased each other past the ends of the earth
You have grown fond of the sound of my feet
Never brave enough to say it
At times you look back
Hoping I would catch up so you can run off again
I often beg my legs to stop
All they ever do is run faster
I would wish my heart would fail
It only gets stronger by the beat
They know one day they will catch you
You know one day you will stop and wait

Golden Days

I would see you every day we didn't have to talk
We were water and oil we didn't have to mix
I was in the dark as the heart nervously saw the light
Back then you were fine, now I can only remember you as
magnificent
I don't know how to feel about those days
Regret blames it on me as if I saw the train coming
Nostalgia saddens me as if the train had arrived by that time
I do wish I had said more
Maybe if I sat closer
We would be cheerfully commemorating the days before the
tide rose
Swallowing up our chances

What is love

To the Wiseman I have a bag of questions
To the ancient of bookkeepers
I ask for the oldest of scrolls
To the songs bird I beg for the most soothing of songs
What is love
Many have paid a heavy price for it
Yet some got it for free
What colour is it
How do you know it is real
People have held on thinking it is real
Others have let go thinking it is fake
How long does it last
Does it fade with time
For others say it only lasted a day
Yet for others its eternal
Who owns love
many never tried it fearing the wrath of its owners
Some told themselves they would never deserve it so who does
This left the Wiseman smiling and thinking
Tried he did but the scroll could not be found
Fearing to sing forever the song bird flew away

Suffering of man

If only we could exchange positions little bird
And I could fly away from what devours my kind
The wind in my feathers would push me higher
For what awaits a man is suffering and more suffering
Life would only be thirteen moons
I would sing to the morning a sweet song so rich and true
Of the tales of man free but not free
Told to me in every visit to him
A life of purpose and meaning is what he seeks
But a dead heart is what he has
Shattered by all the broken dreams
And what kills him the most is hope
The vector of his destruction

Broken

I still felt the pain of each piece
You utterly destroyed my spirit
And left me for dead
I became fool's gold
Undesirable even unto myself
I hid beneath my own shadow never wanting to see my
reflection
Daily I tried myself
Daily I was found guilty
Forever imprisoned in the chambers of regret

Hopeless love

All alone I write countless letters to you
Fully aware you will not get them
So I tell a little bird my words
In the hope it will whisper my whales unto you
I fear pursuing you
Afraid of you outrunning me like you always do
Yet I am afraid of someone else catching you effortlessly

Whispers of the wind

In the ears of a deaf man the wind did whisper
In a language lost and forgotten he heard it all
Pinned down by the weight of the wisdom he had absorbed
The words sunk to the soul
Changing the colour of his eyes
Giving a new shine to his skin
With no one to tell or a home to return to
To a new town he would go
Shouting aloud what had come to him as just whispers

A knock a day

To my face your door was shut
To your face my sky was lit
At your door I still stand, a knock a day
A step outside would change your world forever

Betrayed love

On the banks of hope I waited for your boat
I still bark because you never arrived
Little you gave but much more you took
You never kept me as your own
Instead you got me a longer leash
I thought maybe destiny would bring you back
But to my dismay it wanted you elsewhere
I stand in the rain rejecting your false shelter
Never will I lick your feet
Nor will I howl at your moon
From your path I have chosen to stray

Moonflower

I was alone on the twilight when you spread your petals wide
You weren't shining like the stars of the night's canvas yet u lit
me up inside
A statue is what I then became incapable of movement captured
by life's pierce
You tangled me up with your vines till it was only you the
moonlight found
When day came your bloom was gone yet your ropes held tight
All my friends saw was the cage that held me without a fight
Some tried to cut me free while others pulled me loose for they
misheard my plight
A servant mistaken for a slave was my only crime
Never would I leave your arms
Whether it be day forever
I'm content in your grip
For the slimmest chance to see you at dusk like I did that night

Another reason to come again

I come by your door everyday
My single knock drums in your head
You don't wait to hear my name
You feel my intentions from inside your room
Outside you never come only your tempered voice
Demanding me to go away
The roses in my hand look back at me
They are the reason I came to day
Tomorrow I will buy another reason to come again

Love's Betrayal

You introduced her to me and me to her
You always accompanied us when we met and you passed on my
letters when we were apart
You started the fire and promised to not let it die out
Up the mountains we climbed with you urging us on
When we reached the peak we let out our wings to fly
No storm would blow our way you made sure of it
Even the onlookers noticed your heavy presence
In golden ink you wrote our fairy-tale
Like fireflies on the road's end you guided our every step
Holding each other we would not stumble
On the night of reckoning the cold wind swept our feet
We found ourselves in the dark our fire blown out
We called out to you in the hope you would return to us and be
a part of us like before
We held on to each other for warmth
It turned to clinging as the wind threatened to rip us apart
Disarrayed and hopeless we searched for the path back home
Our own monsters chased us through the dense woods
Exhausted and feet failing I hugged her for the last time
How could we have won
How could we have known the sharp edge of love's betrayal

Shoes that weren't mine

In the place of another I stood and checked
The rooms were larger the window had a crack
Two more steps down the stranger's path and I felt a sweat on
my back
I sighed it was still too early
In my head the voice crept
I didn't have the right tools in this head to conquer the quest
I was who, who was me in this world full of theft
Even she didn't smile at me
I wasn't him
She did her job and swept
This was the final blow inside the man I didn't know
I just wept
Awoken at last from where my head rested on a mat
I'll never take me for granted after this I just can't

Bleeding Heart

Day and night his heart bled
Will was the dagger that poked him from within
Visions robbed him of his sleep
When would his time come was the question he lived with no
answer
The wind pushed him away with the trees waving goodbye
Looking up to the sky that held constellations in the shape of
his success, his only ticket back

War of the heart

Whoever's listening It's not that I enjoy war
But sitting idly I could do no more
Like a car stuck in the highway
I had to do my own tow
My spirit is broken Yes but to say it's the end no
I've been high on my problems I feel so low
Maybe it's destiny's plot to make me my own foe
Like the Baker's rejected dough
Or a warriors broken bow
I've lost and it happens
All I can do is to look at my scar as if it was a big score

Guardian of the night

Too many nights it had seen
Different shades of light it had offered to the blindness of man
Usually at the darkest of his hours
From being a god to just a nightlight
Only the hounds and wolves paid respect to its presence
What annoyed it the most is the arrogance of its pupils
It would peak little by little at their world
Till it was in full light of their deeds
A silent guardian
A handle less torch
An uninvited guest
Watching the world below from the sky above

Children of the mouth

In the happiest of moments I lock my lips
In the saddest of moments I lock my lips
Lest I make anymore children of the mouth
Their giggles sound from afar
An honourable sword in dishonoured hands
At times mocking or praising me their father
Few can be raised well most rebellious and hard to bring up
As debt collectors they were sent for me
Often I did hide when they searched for me
In their numbers they came each one with its own distinctive
cry
Where I left them the people point
begging me to keep them
forcing me to keep them
Away from their faces I go crippled by my inability

Haunted Past

At times I freeze in my tracks
Eyes and mouth wide open
The past pulls me into a black fog
Reintroducing me to the nightmares I dare not relive
Bigger monsters that fortune slew for me
That threaten to come when my luck is low
Ghosts that haunt my mind during the day
Visions of the times when my heart and back were stabbed by
the people I swore to protect
Missteps that sent me flying from the highest of towers
Floods that stole my strongest of bridges
Just when my head is beneath the water
The last and greatest of fears appears
That one day they will call out to me
And I will not answer for my past would have caught up with
me

Pricey Love

I had chased after you for so long
I left my own priorities behind
You charged me a high price for your time
To others years you freely gave
I ordained you a saint and saviour
And declared myself a criminal
I tried sharing my love
but you could never get enough
It was either you or me
You were snow to the desert
Made for someone else

Echoes of silence

I called out to you like I always do

In the echoes of silence my voice was drowned

The heaviness of the darkness brushed off all traces of your light

In my walk alone I slipped on thoughts of you never coming

back

I was falling and not once did I see the bottom

On someone else's shoulders you stood

Whispering the same secrets you told me

Not once did you look back as I cried of the snares you set for

me

The commander

He knew his day had come
He told no one
Alone in the night he strolled from the camp
Death only a pace behind him
What he would leave behind didn't matter
Only the uncertain that was before him
Not only had he lived a life of war
He had become the emblem of war
No salutes would he receive where was going
No gunfire could free him from the clutches of him that held
him
On his knees after he had said his first prayer
His spirit was released into the shadows of the night
He didn't believe his eyes
He that found him
What hope did they have without him
Unrest and commotion befell them
The wise quiet at the news
The foolish restlessly energetic
Was this how their time in arms would end
Sharp knives in the hands of a headless man

Love's light

From the shores of the abandoned island of loneliness I set sail
Eyes like searchlights I never stopped looking
You were a lighthouse to the ship of my heart at the darkest of
hours
With a face that auditioned for so much more
You came to play the part and we were a perfect fit
Like fireflies in a jar you filled my heart
And it let out a glow that even the moon could not ignore

Different worlds

There are different versions of the same world we live in
for the first time I don't know for how long but I'm currently in
another
Where nothing really matters and you do things not for your
own sake but for the sake of those around you
As if u dream the world is just a blur on the reflection of the
stream of life
The conscience no longer speaks because it has run out of words
to tell you
Like a bottomless pit you have quit struggling since you know it
will be like this forever
And you wish u could give it to someone who cares
But there are only reptiles in the place of your habitation

Numbness of life

In the corner of a room I sit
It's not a frown on my face
Do not mistake it for a smile
The treachery of life has diluted the strength of joy
Made numb the pains of sorrow
No longer do I belong among the happy
No longer do I belong among the sad
If to live is to breathe I am alive
But if to live is to live I am dead

What I miss

My reflection on your glasses
The slowing down of the heart
The cooling of my blood
A little lean towards me
The first smile I wish I had seen
The last smile I wish to see
A hug then makes me melt
And you shy away to counter the excitement on my face
Giggling at every bad joke I make
Never differentiating them from the good ones
Lighting up when I call your name
Coming to life when you hear mine
These are the things I miss about you

No room for anyone else

It was never a big room
I would never have thought someone could fit inside
Yet like a mouse you snuck in
Like a whale you made it home
Time chased you away and you left me
Yet in my heart you stayed
Your thoughts never stopped to stalk my mind
And chase me after dark
Coming to life in my sleep
With your presence it continued to grow colder day by day
With only a shadow of you
Who would keep the fire inside burning
If I could invite someone else I would
But with you inside there is no room for anyone else

Beautiful Bloom

A beautiful bloom you were
Everyone knew this
You were the meaning of perfect
You never deserved pruning
Your smile was accompanied by a breeze
That refreshed the entire garden
A Chunk of my time I spent watering you
You decided you loved someone else's water
Your petals grew wider and you shone in a new light
The only part of me I knew you tore off
Leaving me to hold on to thorns

The Day

The hopeful live for the day
The ambitious will ever dream of it
That it does not exist is the fear of the cowards
We can only plan before it arrives
And live it out when it is all over
How high can we jump on the day only the sky knows
How low can we fall only the ground knows
The day awaits us all whether we watch or sleep
The maker and breaker of our lives
The day when fish will fly and birds will swim

The heart's battle

With all advances foiled
The battle became holding my lines
When you eventually came for my walls my heart sank
Looking at the little of myself left I sighed
My heart holding a white flag I staggered to your gates
You marched my dreams to the centre of your city for all to see
And with the swiftness and sharpness of your blade ended it all

Emerald Statue

As days go by I wonder where I'm headed
All alone in a ship that sails itself
And like all ships a reminder of how hallow I am
All alone on the deck pretending I am above it all
I watch the lights of our universe fall dim
The world has been cold for as long as I remember
I am numb
Hope is left just a whisper against the voices of the world
If I'm to be stone let me be emerald a reminder of life
A life green but dead for no stone lives

Love's prey

The predator will always find the prey
Just like how I was found
We don't all have teeth and claws
I wish I did
Is there such a thing as good wolf
Is there such a thing as a bad lamb
Do we choose who we are
If I could I would be you for a change
Eager to see the world from a winner's gaze

You saw a different me

For every cloud you saw rain
Every bump you saw a mountain
Each river was an ocean
Knowing you was knowing me
You believed in me more than I did
And you loved me like you could love no one else
I blame my heart for not agreeing to the trade
I was constantly changing skins yet you held on firmly
I saw your presence as a right
With not enough gratitude and attention to water your flower
It shrunk and love died

I was not me that day

I was not me that day
Boiling in rage shouting at the top of my voice
I did not notice you
There was no space in my mind to put you
While others dodged and ducked the thunder that I shot in all
directions
You stood still
Becoming the first casualty of a stranger's war
The river that streamed from your chicks washed my storm
away
Ashamed of the person we had both witnessed
What apology could save me now
I had met you on the wrong side of me

Lonely Star

Up in the sky they looked at me
A star individually burning through the night
At me alone they looked
How long would I burn in an exchange of a light worth
admiration
With every flare the day approached
The fateful day of depletion

Far away from home

When you want it to rain because inside you it's cloudy
When you wish there was only one song in the world because
that's the one on rewind right now
When you wish people didn't talk about the past because there's
nothing there about you worth talking about
When you wish everyone was like you then everyone would
understand
When your rainbow has been reduced to just blue
When you are wishing for the whole world to cry with you
Go home you are not there yet

The world is cold

I'm not surprised many tried to tell me yes I was told
Is it because my ways and expectations are that of old
But nevertheless this page of my life I shall tear and fold
To think I had direction and I thought I would become the
perfect mould
Where did it come from and where did it go
The feelings that could make a mere mortal so bold
Now I mourn the seconds to hours to days that I sold
A warning to my sisters No it's not only for the old
Pay heed to these words brothers consider yourselves told
The world is not a playground
As you put away your blankets never forget the world is cold

The last fight

In a cold bed he lay
Living and dead at the same time
Pain washed away the numbness he had felt before
And he let out a silent cry
Still pulling in this tug of war against death
A few more breaths he would live
All he could think of was the little flower by his window
The only source of brightness in the room

The option I never had

They always said I had an option
I never did
My heart was a prisoner of hers
With no hope of ever being set free
I was tied to her
But she would never agree to drag me along
They always said I had an option
I never did
The road never got wider
Yet the only one ever bruised was me
I had tried and would continue to try
To pour my soul into her leaking cup

Acknowledgements

I dedicate this book to family and friends who without their help and encouragements this book would die just voices in my head. Extra Special thanks to my uncle Mr E Nyamukachi who brought out the true poet in me.

A special thanks to Zimbabwe as a whole which continues to inspire me to this day.

About the Author

Tinaye Theophany Makwanise is a poet whose verses reflect the rich tapestry of his upbringing in Mutare, Zimbabwe. From the vibrant landscapes of his childhood to the bustling streets of Bulawayo and the serene valleys of Nyanga, Tinaye's poetry is imbued with the essence of his Zimbabwean roots.

A graduate of Masiyephambili Junior School in Bulawayo and St Mary Magdalene's High School in Nyanga, Tinaye continued his academic journey at St Columba's High School, also in Bulawayo, where he completed his A-levels. While his formal education provided a strong foundation, it was his deep-seated passion for poetry that truly shaped his artistic path.

Currently pursuing a course in Electronic Engineering at the Harare Institute of Technology, Tinaye's dual interests in technology and the arts inform his creative endeavors, offering a unique perspective that enriches his poetry.

Tinaye's poetic voice is characterized by its lyrical beauty, introspective depth, and keen observation of the human experience. His verses explore themes of identity, love, loss, and the quest for meaning, inviting readers to journey alongside him through the landscapes of emotion and imagination.

In addition to his writing, Tinaye is an advocate for the power of poetry to inspire change and foster empathy. Through his work, he seeks to bridge divides, celebrate diversity, and ignite conversations that transcend borders and boundaries.